# The Monster Flower Show

*Illustrated by Sally Holmes*

## HAMISH HAMILTON
### LONDON

# HAMISH HAMILTON CHILDREN'S BOOKS

Published by the Penguin Group
27 Wrights Lane, London w8 5TZ, England
Viking Penguin Inc, 40 West 23rd Street, New York, New York 10010, U.S.A.
Penguin Books Australia Ltd, Ringwood, Victoria, Australia
Penguin Books Canada Ltd, 2801 John Street, Markham, Ontario, Canada L3R 1B4
Penguin Books (NZ) Ltd, 182–190 Wairau Road, Auckland 10, New Zealand

Penguin Books Ltd, Registered Offices: Harmondsworth, Middlesex, England

First published in Great Britain 1987 by
Hamish Hamilton Children's Books

Copyright © 1987 by Anne Forsyth
Illustrations copyright © 1987 by Sally Holmes
3 5 7 9 10 8 6 4

British Library Cataloguing in Publication Data

Forsyth, Anne
The monster flower show.—(Gazelle)
I. Title    II. Holmes, Sally
823'.914 [J]    PZ7

ISBN 0-241-12009-8

Filmset in Baskerville by
Katerprint Co. Ltd, Oxford.
Printed and bound in Great Britain at the
University Press, Cambridge

# Chapter One

"Let's enter for the Flower Show!" said Tom.

"What a good idea!" said the teacher.

The children of Colemeadow School were very proud of their garden. They had worked hard.

First they dug over the patch of ground. Then they put in fertiliser to make the soil rich so that the plants would grow well.

Later they raked the soil and sowed the seeds. They watered the little seedlings, and pulled out the weeds.

Now they had lettuces and beans and marrows.

But best of all were the bright yellow sunflowers.

The children couldn't wait to see whose sunflower was the biggest.

"Mine's the tallest one!" said Trevor, who always liked to be first.

But Tom said to himself, "My plant has a bigger flower."

"Listen!" said the teacher next day. "There are special classes in the Show for children. There's a prize for the best decorated cardboard picnic plate: the best six fairy cakes: and listen to this — the largest sunflower bloom."

3

All the children wanted to enter the
Show. As soon as school was over,
they rushed outside to water their
sunflowers. "Go on," said Trevor to
his sunflower, "go on, *grow*!"

On the day of the Show, Tom and
Trevor and all the others cut the
heads from the sunflowers and carefully carried them to the hall where
the Show was to be held. The hall was

4

busy already. On the long trestle tables people were setting out huge onions, giant cabbages and the longest runner beans you ever saw.

Some people were carefully arranging vases of roses and dahlias and mixed flowers. Others carried in their entries for the baking and jam classes — rich, dark chocolate cakes, sausage rolls, jams and pickles.

Tom's dad was helping to run the Show. He was putting up a large banner outside the hall which said, "Flower Show Here Today".

The man at the door gave each of the children a card. On the card was the name of the class: "The largest sunflower bloom", and the child's name.

"That's a fine bloom," he said to Tom. "Going to win a prize?"

Tom put his sunflower on the table with all the others. Then he put his card face downwards beside it. The other children did the same. That meant the judges wouldn't know who each sunflower belonged to. So the judging would be perfectly fair.

"Hm," said Trevor. "I still think my sunflower's the best."

Then the hall was closed while the judges went round with notebooks and pencils. They peered sideways, measured the blooms, looked at them this way and that. Then they wrote on the cards, "FIRST", "SECOND", or "THIRD", or sometimes "HIGHLY COMMENDED", which meant "Not

in the first three but very good all the same".

One of the helpers stuck on the cards the red, blue and green stickers that meant first, second and third prizes, or pink for highly commended.

Soon everything was ready for the Grand Opening of the Show that afternoon. The judges had made their decisions. The exhibitors were anxious to know if their flower or cake or vegetable had won a prize. And everyone wanted to see the displays.

But earlier, when the helpers had nearly finished preparing for the Show, something very unexpected happened.

One of the helpers went out by the back door, his arms full of cardboard boxes. He left the door open.

"Close it behind me, will you?" he shouted.

But no one did.

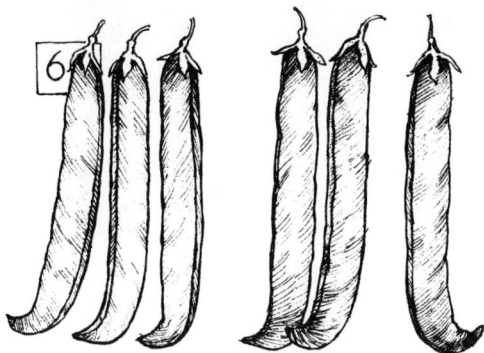

## Chapter Two

Tom's dad was pleased with all the work they'd done. "Come on," he said to Tom, who had been running messages all morning, "that's it for now. Let's get a bite to eat."

"Just a minute before you lock up," said one of the lady helpers. "I left my handbag inside."

She vanished into the hall.

"Eeeeeek!"

"What's that?" said Tom's dad.

"Someone screamed!" said Tom.

Everyone hurried back into the hall. There was the lady just coming out. She clutched the doorpost.

"Oh my! My goodness! What a fright!"

She flopped down on a chair. Someone gave her a glass of water.

"You won't get *me* going back in there," she said after she had sipped it.

"What is it? What's the matter?"

"Matter?" She took a deep breath. "It's a huge beast. Like something from outer space."

"There now," said Tom's dad. "Take it easy."

"Take it easy indeed!" she

snapped. "What are you going to do about it?"

"All right, all right. Let's see what it is. Could be a stoat — or maybe Charlie's ferret has got out again."

Tom followed his dad into the hall and stood, very surprised and pleased.

"It's the monster!"

"What?"

Tom's dad and the others were astonished. "Well, well, would you believe it?"

"It's a baby dinosaur," said Tom.

It was a very strange creature. It had two front legs with five fingers. At the end of the thumb was a kind of sharp spike. It had two long back legs and five stubby toes. Its tail was short

and thick and it was covered all over
with a heavy, scaly sort of skin.

"Remember I told you?" said Tom.
"It came to our school. But you
wouldn't believe me."

"Hallo," said Tom to the dinosaur.
"Hallo, again."

The dinosaur waved its scaly head
from side to side. You would almost
think it was saying, "Hallo".

It was chewing up a pod of runner beans, and it had already eaten half way through a ticket that said "SECOND PRIZE".

"Well, this won't do," said one of the men. "Whatever it is, let's get it out of here fast."

"You chase it out then," said someone else.

"Not me."

"It's a job for the fire brigade."

"Or the police."

"Or the zoo."

Several people backed away.

"It's all right, really," said Tom. He knew a lot about dinosaurs. He collected books about them and had pictures of dinosaurs all over his bedroom wall.

"It's only a baby," he said. "If it was full grown, it would be huge, like a giant. And it's an Iguanodon. They're herbivores — they only eat green things. If it was a carnivore, like Tyrannosaurus Rex, it would eat meat. But this one doesn't. So that's all right."

"No, it's not all right," said Tom's dad. "How can we run a Flower Show if the beast is going to eat the exhibits?"

The dinosaur looked at them, a long runner bean pod sticking out of its mouth. It got to its feet. But it moved only a little further along the hall towards the prize marrows.

"Paper too," said Tom. "They eat paper. Because paper's made from

16

wood pulp and wood pulp comes from trees."

"I know that," said Tom's dad, rather crossly.

"That's why it's eating the prize tickets," Tom went on. The dinosaur was eating a first prize ticket before it started on the marrow.

"I'd like to get this place swept up

before the afternoon," said the caretaker, appearing behind the small
group. "So if you'll just move . . . "

She started to sweep away some
petals that had fallen to the floor.

"What on earth's that?" She sud-
denly saw the dinosaur and stood
very still.

"It's a dinosaur — we think," said
one of the men.

"I don't care what it is," said the

18

caretaker. "It's got no business in my hall. I want it out of here."

The dinosaur had decided that it didn't like marrows. It had moved on to try the prize onions. They were neatly set out — five on a plate.

"Get out — shoo," said the caretaker.

"Go on — out!" said Tom's dad.

"Oh, look," said Tom, "it's crying."

Sure enough, great tears ran down the dinosaur's scaly face.

"You've made it cry," said Tom to the caretaker. "And you," he said to his dad. "Saying you didn't want it here."

"Well, I don't know," said the caretaker, shaking her head.

"It's a shame," said Tom.

"Well, I didn't mean to be unkind," said Tom's dad, who was very fond of animals and always gave the last piece of toast to the dog.

"And *I* didn't mean to be unkind," said the caretaker.

"Nor me," said someone else.

"Of course not," said another.

"Actually," Tom looked more closely at the dinosaur, "I don't think it's really crying. It's the onions . . . "

"So it is!"

"Well, in that case, I'm not going to be sorry for a monster," said the caretaker. "Out you go!" And she pushed the dinosaur with her broom.

The dinosaur opened its jaws and grabbed the broom. It didn't like the

bristles so it spat them out, but it
chewed up the wooden part, every bit.

"Here!" said the caretaker. "That
was a new broom — just a week ago."

"This is serious," said Tom's dad
to the others. "You know what it

means. The beast won't stop at a few onions — "

"A few *prize* onions," said the man who had grown them.

"But if it eats wood," Tom's dad went on, "then it'll eat chairs . . . "

"Tables," said someone else.

"You don't know where it will all end."

The dinosaur lumbered slowly to its feet.

"It's going!" said Tom's dad.

# Chapter Three

But the dinosaur wasn't going. It hopped slowly past the tables, sniffing at the roses as it went.

Then it disappeared into the side hall where the jams and jellies and cakes were on show.

"Quick!"

"Close the door!"

"Call the police!"

Tom's dad went off to phone the police.

"Poor dinosaur!" said Tom to himself. "What will they do to it?"

"Well, what's the trouble?" asked the policeman when he arrived at the hall.

"It's a dinosaur."

"An Iguanodon," said Tom quietly.

"It's in the small hall."

"Let's have a look," said the policeman.

The dinosaur hadn't done *very* much harm. It had eaten the twigs from a flower arrangement which looked a little lopsided now.

It hadn't bothered about the jams and jellies and chutneys.

And it hadn't touched the sausage rolls or scones or cakes — except for one cake.

"A cake for a gardening friend", was the name of the competition.

There were some very good ideas. Some cakes had little houses made of marzipan and flowers of icing sugar, with grated chocolate for earth and paths made of almonds. One had a little pond made from a mirror and toy trees in the garden. The monster had tried one of the trees but had spat it out. Because of course the toy tree was made of plastic and dinosaurs don't eat plastic.

"Hmm," said the policeman. "I think this is a job for the dog handler. I'll just ring the station."

So he spoke into his pocket radio and told the sergeant what had happened.

"Won't be long," he said.

"We open at two," said Tom's dad, getting worried.

"Not to worry," said the policeman. "The dog will see it off. Best dog in the force."

The police dog was a very large Alsatian.

People moved out of his way. You never knew, he might just take a bit out of your leg.

"Where is it then?" asked the dog handler.

By now the dinosaur was asleep. Of course, it had had quite a lot to eat — beans, onions, a flower arrangement,

a broom handle and a prize ticket or two.

It was so deeply asleep that it began to snore. It was a fearsome sound.

The police dog stopped. He lay down on the floor, his head between his paws.

"Get him, boy!" said the handler. "Forward!"

But the dog just lay there and whimpered. Then he turned and slunk out of the hall.

"Well, that's a fine police dog, I must say!" Tom's dad was a bit cross. It had been a long and busy morning, and he wanted his lunch. "Is he scared?"

"'Course he's not scared," said the dog handler. "He's a very good police dog." He didn't like people making rude remarks about his dog. "Show him a burglar or a vandal and he'll be after them — like a shot. But he doesn't know what that is. It didn't come in the training. He didn't do dinosaurs at police college."

"Tell you what," said the first policeman, "we'll get a van and a net. Take him back to the station. Suppose you lock the hall, keep people out meantime. Leave everything to us . . . " And off they went, the two policemen and the dog.

"But the Show opens at two," repeated Tom's dad. He was very worried now. "We can't have a Flower Show with a dinosaur in the midst of it. And if it keeps on eating the vegetables and flowers and prize tickets, we won't have a Show at all. It'll simply vanish."

"I've an idea," said Tom.

# Chapter Four

Tom went into the main hall where all the flowers were on display.

He had been so excited about the dinosaur that he hadn't even looked at the children's classes.

But he knew just where his sunflower was. At the front of the table. And yes, just as he had hoped — there was a large red sticker on his card. First prize.

He stopped. He thought. He gulped.

And then he took his sunflower head and went into the small hall.

He knelt down by the dinosaur and patted it on the head.

"Listen!" he whispered. "They all want you to go. And they're bringing a police van to take you away. I think you had better go before they take you

off to a safari park or a museum, per-
haps. Look!" he went on. "You can
have my sunflower. It's a very good
one."

The dinosaur opened its eyes and
yawned. Tom moved slowly back-
wards out of the door, holding the
sunflower. The dinosaur got to its feet
and hopped after him.

34

Outside the hall, Tom gave his sun-flower to the dinosaur. It nodded its head as if it understood. Then it gob-bled up the sunflower and licked its lips.

Slowly it hopped across the car park and disappeared among the trees, leaving only a few petals behind.

"Well, that's a good thing!" said everyone except Tom.

When the Flower Show opened, people crowded into the hall saying, "Ooh", and "Aah", and "Fancy that — first prize!"

Of course there were a few things missing. People were very surprised.

"Look at that! 'Nine pods of runner beans' it says, and there are only seven. But the judges gave it a first. It's not fair."

"Someone's stolen one of these onions!"

"Look at that flower arrangement. It's all lopsided. But it got a second."

"Well done, Tom," said Tom's teacher. "But where *is* your sunflower?"

"Yes," said Trevor. "Where is it?"

"Well," said Tom, "it was here but, er . . . "

Then it was the prize-giving. All the names of the winners were read out.

"First prize for the biggest sun-flower bloom," said the Show secretary. "Unfortunately Tom's sunflower — er — disappeared. But the judges all said it was the best. It really deserved first prize."

Everyone clapped as Tom went up to get his prize.

"Well done, Tom!"

Some people clapped extra hard, because they knew that Tom had saved the Flower Show. For once an Iguanodon — even a baby Iguanodon

— starts eating green things, there is no stopping it. It might have eaten the whole Flower Show.

Tom shook the envelope he had been given. He could feel the coins inside.

And he knew very well how he was going to spend his prize money.

He was going to buy sunflower seeds for next year. Because the dinosaur liked sunflowers — that was certain.

"Maybe," said Tom to himself, "if I grow sunflowers again next year, the dinosaur will come back for more. You never know."